from SEA TO SHINING SEA

MONTANA

By Judith Bloom Fradin and Dennis Brindell Fradin

◇DIAMOND "P" RANCH◇

CONSULTANTS

Robert Morse Clark, Head, Library and Archives Division, Montana Historical Society

Robert L. Hillerich, Ph.D., Consultant, Pinellas County Schools, Florida; Visiting Professor, University of South Florida

CHILDRENS PRESS®
CHICAGO

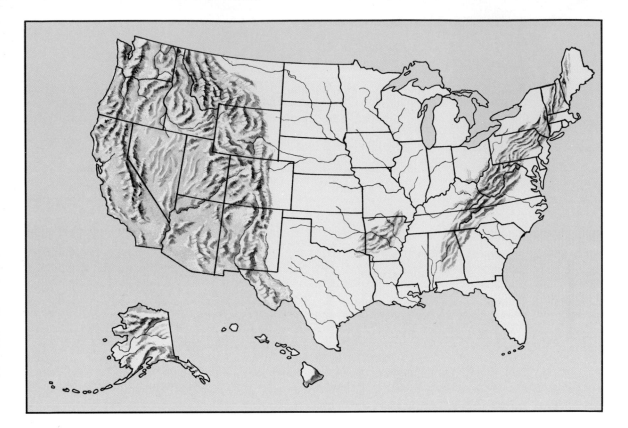

Montana is one of the six Rocky Mountain states. The other Rocky Mountain states are Colorado, Idaho, Nevada, Utah, and Wyoming.

For our children, Anthony, Diana, and Michael

Front cover picture: Haystack Butte, Mt. Gould, Garden Wall, Glacier National Park; page 1: Diamond "P" Ranch, near Gallatin National Park; back cover: a rainbow over a barn at sunset, west of Billings

Project Editor: Joan Downing
Design Director: Karen Kohn
Typesetting: Graphic Connections, Inc.
Engraving: Liberty Photoengraving

THIRD PRINTING, 1994.

Library of Congress Cataloging-in-Publication Data

Fradin, Judith B.
  From sea to shining sea. Montana / by Judith Bloom
Fradin and Dennis Brindell Fradin.
    p. cm.
    Includes index.
    Summary: Discusses the geography, history, industries,
and famous citizens of the "Treasure State."
    ISBN 0-516-03826-5
    1. Montana—Juvenile literature. [1. Montana.] I. Title.
F731.3.F65 1992   91-37958
978.6—dc20   CIP
                                                    AC

Table of Contents

Horses at the North Fork of the Blackfoot River, Flathead Valley

INTRODUCING THE TREASURE STATE

Montana is located in the northwestern United States. The state's name is a Spanish word meaning "mountain." Montana is the fourth-largest of the fifty states. Only Alaska, California, and Texas are larger.

Most of Montana is open plains. Because of its large open spaces, Montana is sometimes called "Big Sky Country." The word "big" fits Montana in many ways. The huge Rocky Mountains cover western Montana. Big ranches and farms make Montana a leading cattle-raising and wheat-growing state. Long ago, giant dinosaurs lived in Montana. In 1876, Montana was the scene of the Battle of the Little Bighorn. This famous battle was fought between American Indians (Native Americans) and the United States Army.

Montana's main nickname is the "Treasure State." In the 1800s, gold was the treasure that drew people to Montana. Today, coal, oil, copper, gold, and silver are mined there. These treasures make Montana a leading mining state.

A picture map of Montana

There is much more that is special about Montana. What state elected the first woman to the United States Congress? Where was movie star Gary Cooper born? Where is Glacier National Park? The answer to these questions is: Montana!

Overleaf: Glacier National Park

From the Mountains

to the Plains

From the Mountains to the Plains

How big is Montana? It is three times the size of the country of England. It is big enough to hold eleven eastern states all at once. They are Connecticut, Delaware, Maine, Maryland, Rhode Island, Vermont, New Hampshire, New Jersey, Massachusetts, South Carolina, and West Virginia.

Montana is one of the six Rocky Mountain states. North and South Dakota border Montana on the east. Wyoming is to the south. Idaho is to the west and southwest. Another country, Canada, is north of Montana.

The five other Rocky Mountain states are Idaho, Wyoming, Colorado, Utah, and Nevada.

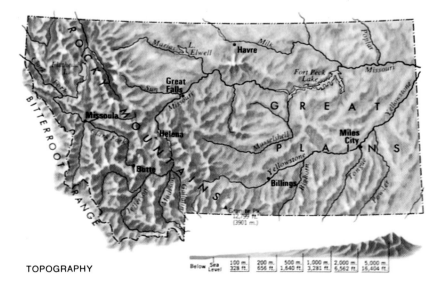

TOPOGRAPHY

TOPOGRAPHY

The Rocky Mountains take up the western two-fifths of Montana. Ranges in Montana's "Rockies" include the Anaconda, Cabinet, Salish, and Flathead mountains. The state's highest peak is in the Rockies. Called Granite Peak, it towers 12,799 feet above sea level. Most of Montana's mines are in the Rockies.

Montana's eastern three-fifths is part of the Great Plains. These are mostly flat, grassy lands. They are broken in places by hills and mountains. Most of Montana's farms and ranches are in the Great Plains region.

St. Mary Lake (left) is in the Rocky Mountains. These wheat fields near Billings (right) are in the Great Plains.

The Yellowstone River, in Paradise Valley

The nation's second-longest river begins in Montana. It is the 2,315-mile-long Missouri River. The source of the Missouri River is near Three Forks. That is where the Jefferson, Madison, and Gallatin rivers come together. The Yellowstone is another important river in Montana. Several major Montana cities lie on or near these rivers. They include Billings, Great Falls, and Helena. Other rivers in Montana include the Bighorn, Little Bighorn, Bitterroot, Flathead, Marias, and Sun.

The Continental Divide runs through Montana's Rocky Mountains. Water from rivers west of the divide end up in the Pacific Ocean.

Water from rivers east of the divide flow to the Atlantic Ocean. Raindrops that fall a few feet apart in Montana can end up thousands of miles apart.

Flathead Lake is in Montana. It is the biggest natural freshwater lake west of the Mississippi River. It covers nearly 200 square miles. Montana also has several artificial lakes. They were made by damming rivers. The largest of these is Fort Peck Lake on the Missouri River. It covers nearly 400 square miles.

About a fourth of Montana is wooded. Important trees include Douglas firs, pines, and cedars. Forests are among the Treasure State's greatest treasures. They are beautiful. They also help make the lumber business important to Montana.

Ferns and violets (left) and Douglas firs (right) grow in Montana's beautiful forests.

CLIMATE

The temperature once dropped to minus 80 degrees Fahrenheit in Alaska.

A mountain lion in a Montana snowstorm

Because Montana is so far north, its winters are cold. January temperatures often dip below 0 degrees Fahrenheit. On January 20, 1954, the temperature fell to minus 70 degrees Fahrenheit. This happened at Rogers Pass, in the Rockies. The only state that has ever been colder is Alaska.

Big winter snowstorms sometimes hit Montana. The Montana Rockies receive several hundred inches of snowfall yearly. On January 20, 1972, 44 inches of snow fell near Glacier National Park. That is the state's largest recorded snowfall for one day.

Montana's summers are often very hot. This is especially true of the Great Plains. July temperatures there often reach above 90 degrees Fahrenheit. Montana's record high temperature was 117 degrees Fahrenheit. This occurred at Glendive on July 20, 1893. It happened again at Medicine Lake on July 5, 1937.

Montana has an unusual weather record. The difference between its hottest and coldest temperature is 187 degrees Fahrenheit. No other state has had that big a temperature difference.

Mountain goats (left) and pelicans (right) are among the wildlife that can be found in Montana.

From Ancient Times Until Today

FROM ANCIENT TIMES UNTIL TODAY

Many millions of years ago, shallow seas covered Montana. Fossils of sea creatures have been found on Montana's mountaintops. The ancient seas helped create the state's oil. Coal was formed in Montana's ancient swamps.

About 75 million years ago, the Rocky Mountains were pushed up out of the earth. Dinosaurs roamed Montana at the time. Tyrannosaurus rex was there. Its teeth were six inches long. Triceratops was there, too. It had three horns on its head. Huge, winged reptiles called pterosaurs ruled the skies.

Montana is a dinosaur hunter's heaven. In 1978, Marion Brandvold of Bynum found a nest of duck-billed dinosaur fossils. In 1988, Montanan Kathy Wankel found a Tyrannosaurus rex skeleton. It is the most complete such skeleton ever found.

THE FIRST PEOPLE

People first reached Montana at least ten thousand years ago. The first Montanans were prehistoric

Montana has the largest deposits of coal of any state.

Opposite: Detail of The Buffalo Runners, an 1890 painting by C.M. Russell

15

White Man Runs Him (above) was a Crow who acted as a scout for George Armstrong Custer.

Artist Frederic Remington made this drawing of Sioux Indians who lived on the eastern plains of Montana.

Indians. They hunted giant bison and other animals with spears. About one thousand years ago, American Indians invented the bow and arrow.

Before any Europeans arrived, many American Indian groups lived in Montana. The Arapaho, Blackfeet, Crow, Cheyenne, and Assiniboine lived on the eastern plains. They hunted bison, often called buffalo. They ate its meat. They made clothes and tepees from bison skins. The Sioux came to Montana from the Dakotas to hunt.

Other groups lived in Montana's Rockies. They included the Kutenai, Shoshone, Salish, and Bannock. The mountain people hunted deer and bears. They also fished and gathered berries.

FUR TRAPPERS AND EXPLORERS

France sent explorers to Canada in the early 1600s. French fur traders followed. They traded goods with the Indians. In return, they got beaver fur and other furs. The furs were shipped to Europe to be made into clothing. In time, the French Canadians grew curious about lands to the south. They became the first non-Indians to reach Montana.

Two French-Canadian brothers were the first known non-Indians in Montana. Their names were

François and Louis Joseph de La Vérendrye. They were hunting for new sources of furs. From the Vérendryes' work, France claimed Montana. But the French did not settle the region.

François de La Vérendrye (above) and his brother Louis Joseph were the first known non-Indians in Montana.

In 1776, a new nation was born in America—the United States. At first, the country was limited to the East Coast. Then, in 1803, the United States bought the Louisiana Territory from France. Most of Montana was part of the Louisiana Territory. It did not become a state for many years.

Americans wanted to learn more about their new lands. In 1804, President Thomas Jefferson sent two men west to explore them. They were

Captains Meriwether Lewis and William Clark. Sacagawea, a young Indian woman, helped Lewis and Clark. During the long trip, Sacagawea carried her baby, Pomp, on her back. A 200-foot-tall rock in southeastern Montana is called Pompey's Pillar. Clark named it for Sacagawea's son.

Two highways follow much of Lewis and Clark's route through Montana. U.S. Highway 2 follows part of the explorers' westward trip through Montana. Interstate 90/94 follows Clark's return trip home through Montana.

Lewis and Clark saw that Montana was rich in furs. Soon, fur companies built trading posts and forts there. In 1807, Manuel Lisa built Montana's first fur-trading post. It was at the mouth of the

In 1807, artist C. M. Russell painted this picture of Captain William Clark of the Lewis and Clark Expedition meeting with the Indians of the Northwest.

Bighorn River. He named it Fort Manuel. Then, fur traders and trappers arrived. The trappers caught beavers and other animals. The traders got the furs from the Indians.

The trappers and traders were tough men. One of them was John Colter. He was captured by Blackfeet. The Blackfeet let Colter run for his life. He ran from present-day Three Forks, Montana, to Fort Manuel. Hundreds of Indians chased him. But Colter traveled the 200 miles to the fort in one week.

By 1850, most of Montana's fur-bearing animals were gone. The great days of the fur trade in Montana were over. But soon another treasure drew thousands of people to Montana.

French-Canadian fur trappers such as this one arrived in Montana in the early 1800s.

GOLD

Gold was found in California in 1848. People began to search for gold elsewhere. Around 1860, a few miners found small amounts of gold in Montana. In July 1862, John White struck gold at Grasshopper Creek.

The news spread. Within a few days, five hundred miners had reached Grasshopper Creek. In 1863, an even bigger strike was made nearby.

Fort Union (above) was one of Montana's many fur-trading posts.

Above: The mining camp at Grasshopper Creek became the town of Bannack.

Below: The Cavitt brothers were among the miners who came to Montana in the 1860s.

Virginia City was begun at that site. Within two years, Virginia City was home to ten thousand people.

In 1864, other miners were looking for gold. They called their camp Last Chance Gulch. They planned to give up if they didn't find gold there. But the men struck it rich. The town of Helena was begun at Last Chance Gulch that year.

Butte was another town that began as a gold camp in 1864. Huge amounts of silver and copper were also found in Butte. The town became one of the leading mining areas in North America.

Life was rough in the mining towns. Miners fought with their fists in saloons. Now and then, there were gunfights. Outlaws were also a problem. Henry Plummer was a special problem. He headed a gang that robbed stagecoaches, but he was also the sheriff. In 1863, Plummer's gang killed more than one hundred people. Finally, Montanans took the law into their own hands. They hanged Henry Plummer in January 1864. They also hanged more than twenty other robbers. This helped end the robberies and murders.

Other people besides miners moved to Montana during the 1860s. Families opened stores in the mining towns. A few cattle ranchers arrived.

Montana's first two schools were begun in 1863. Lucia Darling ran one of them in Bannack. Kate Dunlap taught in Nevada City at the other school.

The mining boomtown of Helena (above) as it looked in 1865

In 1863, Congress created the Idaho Territory. Montana was part of this territory. By 1864, most people in the Montana region wanted Montana to become a separate territory. This would start Montana on the road toward statehood. It would also give Montana a better government. The United States Congress made Montana a territory on May 26, 1864. Sidney Edgerton was the Montana Territory's first governor.

MONTANA'S INDIAN WARS

Not everyone was happy about Montana's growth. The American Indians were suffering. In 1837, more than ten thousand Blackfeet and Assiniboine died of smallpox. White traders may have given them the disease. Later, white settlers took the Indians' land in Montana and other western states. White hunters had also killed millions of bison. This destroyed a major source of food for the Indians. Some of the Indians fought to save their way of life.

Bozeman, Montana, was named for John Bozeman.

From 1863 to 1864, John Bozeman blazed a trail from Wyoming to Virginia City, Montana. It was called the Bozeman Trail. It cut through Indian land. Sioux and Cheyenne attacked settlers who followed the trail. Bozeman himself was killed in an attack by Blackfeet. The Indians also attacked forts built to protect the settlers.

Reservations are lands set aside for American Indians.

The United States government ordered Montana's Indians onto reservations in 1875. This opened more Indian land to settlement. Troops were sent to force the Sioux and Cheyenne onto reservations.

The troops destroyed a Cheyenne camp along Montana's Powder River in March 1876. Sioux chief Crazy Horse formed and led a Sioux and Cheyenne army. That force defeated United States troops on June 17, 1876, along Rosebud Creek.

Eight days later, on June 25, 1876, a more famous battle occurred. Lieutenant Colonel George Custer attacked an Indian village along the Little Bighorn River. Why he did this is a mystery. Custer had fewer than three hundred men. The Indians had thousands of warriors. They fought under such great leaders as Sitting Bull and Chiefs Crazy Horse and Gall. Custer and the men with him were killed at the Battle of the Little Bighorn. The battle became known as Custer's Last Stand.

George Armstrong Custer (above) and his troops were killed at the Battle of the Little Bighorn (below).

Later, the Sioux and Cheyenne were defeated in and near Montana. Then, in 1877, the Nez Percé were fleeing through Montana. They hoped to reach Canada. Just 30 miles from Canada, United States troops surrounded them. The Nez Percé fought, but soon had to surrender. Chief Joseph, the Nez Percé leader, made a famous surrender speech. "The little children are freezing to death," he said. "My heart is sick and sad. From where the sun now stands, I will fight no more forever." Chief Joseph's surrender marked the end of Montana's Indian wars. By 1880, nearly all of Montana's Native Americans were on reservations.

THE FORTY-FIRST STATE

Montana enjoyed great growth during the 1880s. Mining boomed. In 1881, Marcus Daly hit Montana's richest copper deposit. In 1885 alone, gold, silver, and copper brought in $21 million. In 1891, Daly founded the giant Anaconda Copper Mining Company.

Montana was also one of the nation's leading ranching regions by then. Cowboys tended the cattle. Twice a year, they rounded up the cattle. In the spring, they branded the calves. In that way, every-

These men worked in an underground copper mine in Butte.

one knew which ranch owned them. In the fall, the cowboys herded the cattle to market. By 1886, Montana ranches and farms were home to seven hundred thousand cattle. They also had about a million sheep.

Railroads reached Montana during the 1880s. Trains and wagons brought more families to Montana. In 1884, Montanans asked the United States Congress for statehood. The territory had more than one hundred thousand people by the late 1880s. Congress finally made Montana the forty-first state on November 8, 1889. Helena was the capital, as it still is.

Thousands of people moved to the new state. Many came from other states. Some arrived from Germany, Norway, and Sweden. Many of them

Cattle ranches and sheep ranches such as these made Montana a leading ranching region by the 1880s.

25

started wheat farms and cattle ranches. Between 1910 and 1920, Montana's population rose from 376,053 to 548,889 people.

WORLD WARS AND DEPRESSION

A Montanan achieved an important "first" in 1916. Her name was Jeannette Rankin. In November 1916, she was elected to the United States House of Representatives. Rankin was the first woman member of Congress. She became famous for her hatred of war.

In 1917, the United States entered World War I (1914-1918). Rankin voted against entering the

Jeannette Rankin (right) was the first woman member of the United States Congress.

26

war. More than forty-one thousand Montanans served during the war.

Montana suffered some hard times after the war. A period of little rainfall hit Montana in 1917. This is known as a drought. There were several droughts in the 1920s. Crops dried up, badly hurting Montana's farmers. A business slump that struck the whole nation in 1929 made things worse. It began the Great Depression. The depression lasted ten years. Factories closed. Farmers had to sell their farms. Mines closed. By 1935, a quarter of all Montanans were receiving relief money. This money came from the United States government.

Government projects helped Montanans survive the hard times. The government hired people to build roads and dams. The dams provided water for farmers. They also helped produce electricity for the state. About ten thousand workers built Fort Peck Dam on the Missouri River. It took them six years (1934-1940) to build it.

Conditions improved in Montana around 1939. That year, World War II (1939-1945) began. About fifty-seven thousand Montanans helped the United States and its allies win. Montana's farms and ranches provided wheat and beef for the troops. Montana's copper went into airplanes.

During World War II, Montana governor Sam Ford's wife prepared packages for soldiers.

Recent Growth and Problems

During the 1950s, major oil fields were discovered. Oil wells were drilled along the Montana-North Dakota border. The oil industry grew in importance in Montana. During the 1970s, coal mining became very important to the Treasure State.

From 1965 to 1973, the United States fought a war in Asia. Large numbers of Americans opposed this Vietnam War. Two Montanans were among the antiwar leaders. One was United States senator Mike Mansfield. The other was Jeannette Rankin. In 1968, Rankin led a march in Washington, D.C. She and five thousand other women protested the war. The women called themselves the Jeannette Rankin Brigade. In this way, they honored their eighty-seven-year-old leader.

During the 1980s, Montana again suffered some hard times. Profits from copper mining fell. The huge Anaconda firm closed its mining operations in Butte in 1983. This cost thousands of Montanans their jobs. Oil prices fell, hurting the state's oil business. A drought during the 1980s was a blow to farmers and ranchers.

Montana celebrated its one-hundredth birthday as a state in 1989. But because of these troubles, it

wasn't a very happy one. In fact, thousands of families were leaving Montana. Between 1985 and 1990, the population dropped from about 826,000 to 779,000. In 1990, seven of every one hundred Montana adults had no work. Only a handful of states had a larger percentage of jobless people.

Montanans are working to make their state's 110th birthday in 1999 happier. Montana is trying to attract more out-of-state visitors. This would bring millions of dollars into the state. Montana is also trying to attract more industry and mining. This would provide jobs for out-of-work people.

During Montana's centennial celebration in 1989, an 1889 cattle drive was reenacted.

Montanans and Their Work

MONTANANS AND THEIR WORK

The United States Census reported that Montana had 799,065 people in 1990. Only Wyoming, Alaska, Vermont, North Dakota, Delaware, and South Dakota have fewer people.

Montana is big, but it has few people. In fact, Montana has only five people per square mile. Several eastern states have nearly one thousand people per square mile. Because Montanans are few and far between, they tend to value each person's independence. They also take pride in being friendly.

Nearly fifty thousand Native Americans live in Montana. Few states have more. The Blackfeet, Salish, Kutenai, Northern Cheyenne, Sioux, Assiniboine, Crow, and Cree are among Montana's Indian nations. Most of the state's Indians live on seven reservations. Some live in towns and cities around the state. They work as farmers, ranchers, office workers, and miners.

Montanans tend to be older than other Americans. They are also better educated. Montana's literacy rate is very high. This means that almost all of its people can read and write.

Montana has only five people per square mile.

Opposite: A Blackfoot boy dressed for a ceremony eating a sno-cone

There are three cattle for each person in Montana.

Service jobs employ the most people in Montana. About 113,000 Montanans provide services. They include doctors, nurses, and people who run stores and hotels.

Government work employs the second-largest number of people. About eighty thousand Montanans have government jobs. One reason for this is the state's many parks, forests, and Indian reservations.

About thirty-one thousand Montanans work on farms and ranches. Montana has 2.5 million beef cattle. That makes it a leading cattle-raising state. It has six hundred thousand sheep. That makes it a top sheep-raising state. Montana is also among the top five states for growing wheat and barley. Other farm products include milk, sugar beets, hogs, cherries, potatoes, and hay. Millions of Americans use another Montana product each December. The state is a leading grower of Christmas trees.

More than twenty thousand Montanans work in factories. Forest products are the state's leading kind of manufactured goods. These include lumber and paper. Food packaging is also important. Food companies turn Montana wheat into flour. Sugar beets become packaged sugar.

About seven thousand people help make Montana a leading mining state. Oil and coal are Montana's top mining products today. Montana ranks about thirteenth in the nation at pumping oil. It is about eighth at mining coal. Only about four states mine more gold than the Treasure State. Montana is also a major producer of copper, silver, lead, and natural gas.

Overleaf: A log cabin in the Beartooth Mountains

Beet farmers (left) and park rangers (right) are among the people who live and work in Montana.

A Trip Through Montana

A Trip Through Montana

Each year, more than five million people visit Montana. They come to see the Rocky Mountains. They explore the battlefield where Crazy Horse and George Custer fought. They visit Montana's small but interesting cities and towns.

Southeastern Montana

William Clark named this rock Pompey's Pillar in honor of Sacagawea's son.

Southeastern Montana is a big coal-mining area. It is also the site of Montana's largest city. Billings was founded in 1882 when a railroad was built through the region. Billings is now a shipping center. Sugar beets, meat, wheat, and vegetables are packed there.

Pictograph Cave State Historical Site is near Billings. Pictographs are drawings made on rock walls. A trail leads to the drawings at the cave. Indians made the drawings beginning about two thousand years ago. Tools about eight thousand years old have been found at the cave.

Following the Yellowstone River east from Billings leads to Pompey's Pillar. Captain William Clark climbed this 200-foot-tall rock on July 25,

1806. He carved his name on the rock. Petrified wood can also be seen in places along the Yellowstone. This is wood that has turned to stone over the ages.

The Crow Indian Reservation is south of Pompey's Pillar. It is Montana's largest reservation. It is home to most of the country's eighty-five hundred Crow. Each August, the Crow Fair is held on the reservation. This is a special time when the Crow recall their heritage. The Crow raise more than a thousand tepees for the fair. For a week, they live in the tepees. They perform dances and hold horseback-riding contests.

Custer Battlefield National Monument is on the Crow Reservation. Custer and his men were killed there while attacking the Sioux and Cheyenne.

Left: The city of Billings is on the Yellowstone River. Right: The Crow Fair is the largest gathering of American Indians in the United States.

About 150 miles northeast of the battlefield is Medicine Rocks State Park. These sandstone rocks have strange shapes. Wind and water have carved them over the ages. The Indians considered the rocks a holy place.

NORTHEASTERN MONTANA

About 150 miles north of Medicine Rocks is Fort Peck Indian Reservation. Sioux leader Sitting Bull surrendered near where the reservation now stands. Today, Assiniboine and Sioux live on the reservation. Each July, the Wild Horse Stampede is held at Wolf Point. This town is on the reservation. The stampede was first held in 1901.

These columns of rock in Makoshika State Park are called hoodoos.

Several wildlife refuges are near the reservation. Medicine Lake Refuge is home to many birds. Hawks, pelicans, whooping cranes, owls, and geese can be seen there. Charles Russell Refuge is home to deer, elk, bighorn sheep, and antelope. Paddlefish also live within the Russell Refuge. They are an ancient fish. Their noses look something like paddles or oars.

Fort Peck Dam is also near the reservation. The Fort Peck Museum is at the dam. Visitors can learn how this 4-mile-wide dam was built. They also can see fossils that have been found in the area.

Fort Peck Lake is a big fossil-hunting area. That is where Kathy Wankel found the Tyrannosaurus rex skeleton.

Besides fossils, northeastern Montana has many wheat farms, ranches, and oil wells. It is one of the nation's top wheat-growing areas. The wheat is used to make bread and breakfast cereals. Sheep and cattle are also raised in the region. Some of Montana's richest oil deposits are found there, too.

Northeastern Montana has few people and no large cities. The largest city in this part of the state is Havre. It has just about ten thousand people.

East of Havre is Bears Paw Battlefield. The Nez Percé fought United States troops there for four

The Charles Russell Wildlife Refuge is home to many kinds of animals, including elk (above).

days. On October 5, 1877, the Nez Percé surrendered. That was when Chief Joseph said, "I will fight no more forever."

NORTHWESTERN MONTANA

One of Montana's oldest towns is a short drive from Bears Paw Battlefield. This is Fort Benton. It began as a fort in 1846. The old fort's ruins can be seen in the town. Fort Benton also has a wonderful outdoor sculpture. It shows Lewis and Clark with Sacagawea.

Fort Benton is on the Missouri River. About 50 miles southwest of Fort Benton is a waterfall. It is called the Great Falls of the Missouri. In 1883, a town was begun at the Great Falls. Called Great Falls, it is now Montana's second-biggest city.

Concrete and flour are made in Great Falls. Malmstrom Air Force Base near Great Falls employs many of the city's people. Western artist Charles M. Russell lived in Great Falls. The C. M. Russell Museum in the city shows many of his works.

Long ago, the Indians killed bison by driving them off pishkuns. These are high cliffs. Ulm Pishkun is near Great Falls. This is a 50-foot-high cliff. It is thought to be the country's largest

Pawnee Chief *(above), a 1907 watercolor by Charles M. Russell, is part of the collection at the C. M. Russell Museum in Great Falls.*

40

pishkun. Indians used this pishkun more than a thousand years ago. Tools that old have been found there.

Avalanche Lake is one of the many lakes in Glacier National Park.

Giant Springs is also near Great Falls. Springs are waters that bubble out of cracks in the ground. Giant Springs is one of the largest freshwater springs on earth.

An unusual national park is in northwestern Montana at the Canadian border. It is called Glacier National Park. There are about fifty glaciers in the park. They were formed near the end of the Ice

Age. Montana's long, cold winters keep them from melting. The park also has towering mountains and hundreds of waterfalls. Iceberg Lake is one of the park's prettiest lakes. It contains icebergs even in July.

Many people go to Glacier National Park just to see the wildlife. Moose, bighorn sheep, mountain goats, elk, mountain lions, and black bears live in the park. Grizzly bears, coyotes, and even a few wolves can be seen in places. Bald eagles can also be spotted. The bald eagle is America's national bird.

Southwest of Glacier National Park is the National Bison Range. One of the country's last big bison herds lives there. In the mid-1800s, millions

Sights in Glacier National Park include a natural drinking fountain on Grinnell Glacier (left) and Iceberg Lake (right).

of bison lived in America. By the late 1800s, hunters had killed nearly all of them. Today, about five hundred bison feed on the range's grasslands.

Montana's third-biggest city isn't far from the bison range. This is Missoula. It was settled in 1860. Missoula's name comes from an Indian word meaning "near the chilling waters." Lumber, meat, and paper are produced in Missoula.

The University of Montana is in Missoula. The city is also the largest base for the United States Forest Service smoke jumpers. The smoke jumpers are flown over the sites of forest fires. They parachute down to fight the fires.

Left: The University of Montana, in Missoula Right: Bison at the National Bison Range, southwest of Glacier National Park

The University of Montana's sports teams are called the Grizzlies.

SOUTHWESTERN MONTANA

Cattle branding at the Grant-Kohrs Ranch National Historic Site

Southwestern Montana is a big ranching area. Today, cowboys and ranchers often work from trucks. But many of them still work on horseback. There is a famous ranch on the outskirts of Deer Lodge. It is called the Grant-Kohrs Ranch National Historic Site. Visitors can learn how cowboys lived and worked in the 1800s.

Montana's capital is east of the ranch. At the town's founding in 1864, miners called it Last Chance Gulch. But within weeks, they changed the name to Helena. With almost twenty-five thousand people, Helena is now Montana's fifth-largest city. Food, bricks, and metals are made in and near Helena.

Helena has reminders of its roots. One of its main streets is called Last Chance Gulch. The street was built where the first gold was discovered. Pioneer Cabin in Helena dates from the year the town was founded.

Helena has been Montana's capital since 1875. Visitors can tour the state capitol. Montana's law-makers meet there. The building's copper dome rises to a height of 165 feet. A statue that stands for Liberty is on top of the dome.

The Montana Historical Society is also in Helena. Works by Montana artist Charles M. Russell are displayed there. Henry Plummer's shotgun and Chief Joseph's stirrups can also be seen.

Montana has a number of "ghost towns." These towns were built when miners entered an area. They died when the miners left. Two interesting ghost towns are west of Helena. At Garnet, the remains of an 1870s gold-mining town can be seen. At Granite, buildings from an 1880s silver-mining settlement still stand. There are also some sapphire mines near Helena. Visitors can dig for sapphires and other gems. They can keep what they find.

Left: The state capitol, in Helena
Right: Last Chance Gulch is one of Helena's main streets.

The sapphire is one of Montana's state stones.

Butte is 60 miles southwest of Helena. It is pronounced "beaut," like "beauty" without the "y." Founded in 1864, Butte was named for Big Butte. This is a nearby volcanic mountain. A butte is a steep mountain or hill that rises sharply above the nearby land.

Butte has been called the "Richest Hill on Earth." Between 1864 and 1983, 20 billion pounds of copper were mined there. The copper went into such items as coins, wire, and pots and pans. During that time, 60 million pounds of silver were mined in Butte. Also, 240,000 pounds of gold were mined there. Mining declined after 1940. But it is still important to Butte.

A restored one-room school in Nevada City

Visitors can view open-pit copper mines in Butte. Berkeley Pit is a copper-mining pit there. It is half a mile deep. Huge homes belonging to Montana's "copper kings" can also be seen in Butte. William A. Clark's mansion has thirty rooms. Clark and Marcus Daly were copper-mining rivals.

Virginia City is about 60 miles south of Butte. Virginia City has been restored to look as it did in 1865. Nearby is Robbers' Roost. Henry Plummer and his gang planned their holdups there. Five gang members were hanged in Virginia City. They were buried at Virginia City's Boot Hill Cemetery.

About 80 miles east of Butte is Bozeman. Bozeman was founded in 1864. It is home to Montana State University. The Museum of the Rockies is part of this school.

Yellowstone National Park would be a good place to end a Montana trip. The park is about 50 miles south of Bozeman. It is the nation's oldest national park. Yellowstone is a region of hot springs, canyons, and waterfalls. Nearly all of the park is in Wyoming. Small parts of the park are in Montana and Idaho. Three of the park's five entrances are in Montana. The Museum of the Yellowstone is a good place to learn about the park. It is in West Yellowstone, Montana.

This old storefront is in Virginia City, an old mining town that has been restored.

Montana State University's sports teams are called the Bobcats.

A Gallery of Famous Montanans

A Gallery of Famous Montanans

Montana is a state with a small population. But it has been home to many famous people. They include Native American leaders, lawmakers, scientists, and actors.

Pierre-Jean De Smet (1801-1873) was born in Belgium. He came to America when he was twenty. De Smet became a Catholic priest and missionary. He worked for many years among the western Indians. In 1841, Father De Smet built St. Mary's Mission near present-day Stevensville. There, he planted wheat, oats, and potatoes. Those were the first crops grown by non-Indians in Montana. Father De Smet kept peace between Montana's Indians and settlers for many years.

Sacagawea (1789?-1812?) was born in Idaho. She was a Shoshone. As a child, she lived in Montana near present-day Three Forks. One night, Hidatsa Indians raided Sacagawea's village. She was taken as a slave to North Dakota. There, French trader Toussaint Charbonneau bought her from the Hidatsa. Charbonneau forced Sacagawea to marry him. They were living in North Dakota when Lewis

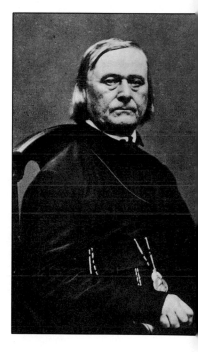

Missionary Pierre-Jean De Smet

Opposite: Congresswoman Jeannette Rankin

and Clark passed through. In 1805, Sacagawea, her baby Pomp, and Charbonneau went with the explorers. Sacagawea helped Lewis and Clark on the trip to the Pacific Ocean. For her service, she received a Jefferson peace medal.

Crazy Horse (1849-1877) was born in a Sioux village. No one knows the exact place. Crazy Horse's greatest fame came in 1876 in Montana. He defeated George Custer at the Battle of the Little Bighorn. A year later, Crazy Horse surrendered in Nebraska. A soldier stabbed him to death soon after.

Marcus Daly (1841-1900) was born in Ireland. At the age of fifteen, he moved to the United States. Daly worked as a miner in California and Nevada. Then, in 1876, a mining company sent him to Butte. He bought a mine there. While exploring the mine, Daly struck a huge copper vein. This was the start of Montana's copper industry. Daly started the Anaconda Copper Mining Company in 1891. He used some of his riches to found the city of Anaconda. He also built banks and a railroad in Montana.

Mary Fields (1832-1914) was born a slave in Tennessee. By the 1880s, she had moved to Montana. She settled near Cascade and became a

Copper-mine owner Marcus Daly

stagecoach driver. For eight years, Mary Fields delivered the mail in Montana. She was the second woman in the country to deliver the U.S. mail. She had to be strong to do that. She once beat a man in a gunfight.

Charles Marion Russell (1864-1926) was born in St. Louis, Missouri. As a child, he loved to draw pictures of cowboys. At the age of sixteen, he visited Montana. He loved it so much that he moved there. Russell worked as a cowboy for many years. He made hundreds of paintings and sculptures of what he saw.

Jeannette Rankin (1880-1973) was born near Missoula. She grew up on a Montana ranch. She went to the University of Montana. After graduating, she taught school. But politics became her chief love. Rankin helped convince Montana lawmakers to allow women to vote in 1914. Two years later, Montanans elected her the first woman in Congress. Rankin first served in the U.S. House of Representatives from 1917 to 1919. She served again from 1941 to 1943. She voted against the nation's entry into World War I and World War II. She was the only member of Congress to vote against both of those wars. Rankin lived to be almost ninety-three years old.

This statue of artist Charles M. Russell is in Great Falls.

Actor Gary Cooper

Writer A. B. Guthrie

Gary Cooper (1901-1961) was born in Helena. He tended cattle on his family's ranch. This helped him later when he became a movie star. Cooper often played cowboy heroes. His films include *High Noon*, *The Westerner*, and *Sergeant York*.

Some people say that *High Noon* is the greatest Western film ever made. Others give the honor to *Shane*. Either way, a Montanan was involved. Around the time that Gary Cooper was making *High Noon*, **A. B. Guthrie** was writing the script for *Shane*. Guthrie (1901-1991) was born in Indiana. When he was six months old, his family moved to Montana. He lived there most of his life. Guthrie's western novels include *The Big Sky* and *The Way West*.

Mike Mansfield was born in New York City in 1903. He moved to Montana at the age of three. Mansfield joined the U.S. Navy when he was not quite fifteen. He was the youngest Montana man to serve during World War I. After the war, he finished his schooling and graduated from the University of Montana. He taught history there from 1933 to 1942. In the early 1940s, Mansfield began a career in politics. He became one of the most famous law-makers in Montana's history. Mansfield served in the U.S. House of Representatives for ten years (1943-1953). He served in the U.S. Senate for twenty-four years (1953-1977). He helped lower America's voting age to eighteen. He also worked to protect the rights of blacks. Mansfield later served as the U.S. ambassador to Japan (1977-1988).

A Montana woman helped save thousands of children's lives around the world. Her name was **Grace Eldering** (1900-1988) and she was born in Myers. Grace Eldering became a doctor. She and a friend, Dr. Pearl Kendrick, searched for a way to prevent whooping cough. They created a vaccine against this disease in 1939. Later, they created the DTP shot. It protects against diphtheria, tetanus, and whooping cough.

Senator Mike Mansfield

Whooping cough is sometimes called pertussis. The "p" in DTP stands for pertussis.

The birthplace of Dr. Grace Eldering, Jeannette Rankin, and Gary Cooper . . .

The home of Mike Mansfield, Charles Russell, and Father De Smet . . .

A leading state for mining, cattle ranching, and wheat growing . . .

A land of big skies, big mountains, big ranches, and big dinosaur bones . . .

The first state to send a woman to the U.S. Congress . . .

This is Montana—the Treasure State!

Did You Know?

In 1989, a gold nugget weighing about 2 pounds was found near Butte. It is the largest known gold nugget found in Montana during the last eighty years. The nugget is displayed at the Mineral Museum in Butte.

Millions of people have seen the Tyrannosaurus rex skeleton in New York City's American Museum of Natural History. It was found on a ranch that is now under Montana's Fort Peck Dam.

The Crow Indians asked Father Pierre-Jean De Smet to walk up to a bison to prove that he was a holy man. It is said that Father De Smet calmly walked up to the huge animal, patted its head, then returned unharmed to the Indians.

Montana ranchers eagerly await the *chinook* so that their cattle can graze. The *chinook* is a warm wind that melts snow in the winter and early spring. The Blackfeet call it "the snow eater."

Glacier National Park is home to sixty kinds of mammals, two hundred kinds of birds, and twelve hundred kinds of plants. An eagle's nest 8 feet by 20 feet and weighing 4,000 pounds was once found there.

Eureka calls itself the "Christmas Tree Capital of the World." The town produces hundreds of thousands of Christmas trees each year.

In late 1935, Helena was rocked by hundreds of earthquakes. Damage was heavy, but only a few people died.

Helen Peterson's sixth-grade class in Livingston worked to make the duck-billed dinosaur the state fossil. The students wrote letters and attended state hearings. They even served "dinosaur" cookies in the state capitol. On February 22, 1985, Governor Ted Schwinden went to Mrs. Peterson's class to sign a bill making the duck-billed dinosaur the state fossil.

The world's greatest known temperature change in a twenty-four-hour period occurred at Browning, on January 23-24, 1916. The temperature dropped 100 degrees from 44 degrees Fahrenheit to minus 56 degrees Fahrenheit.

Montana has more than 100 of the nation's 640 one-room schoolhouses. Some have only four or five students.

Large numbers of frozen grasshoppers can be seen in Grasshopper Glacier, near Granite Peak, in southwestern Montana. Long ago, the grasshoppers fell into the glacier and were frozen in the ice.

55

Montana Information

The state flag

Bitterroot

Western meadowlark

Area: 147,046 square miles (fourth among the states in size)

Greatest Distance North to South: 321 miles

Greatest Distance East to West: 559 miles

Borders: North Dakota and South Dakota to the east; Wyoming to the south; Idaho to the west and southwest; the Canadian provinces of British Columbia, Alberta, and Saskatchewan to the north

Highest Point: Granite Peak in the Rocky Mountains, 12,799 feet above sea level

Lowest Point: 1,800 feet above sea level (along the Kootenai River in northwestern Montana)

Hottest Recorded Temperature: 117°F. (at Glendive, on July 20, 1893, and again at Medicine Lake, on July 5, 1937)

Coldest Recorded Temperature: -70°F. (at Rogers Pass, on January 20, 1954)

Statehood: The forty-first state, on November 8, 1889

Origin of Name: *Montana* means "mountain" in Spanish

Capital: Helena (since 1875)

Previous Capitals: Bannack and Virginia City

Counties: 56

United States Senators: 2

United States Representatives: 1 (as of 1992)

State Senators: 50

State Representatives: 100

State Song: "Montana," by Charles C. Cohen (words) and Joseph E. Howard (music)

State Motto: *Oro y Plata* (Spanish, meaning "Gold and Silver")

Nicknames: "Treasure State," "Big Sky Country," "Land of the Shining Mountains"

Grizzly bears

State Seal: Adopted in 1893

State Flag: Adopted in 1905

State Flower: Bitterroot

State Bird: Western meadowlark

State Tree: Ponderosa pine

State Animal: Grizzly bear

State Fish: Black-spotted cutthroat trout

State Gemstones: Sapphire and agate

State Fossil: Duck-billed dinosaur

Main Mountain System: Rocky Mountains

Some Rivers: Missouri, Yellowstone, Jefferson, Madison, Gallatin, Bighorn, Little Bighorn, Tongue, Powder, Kootenai, Teton, Marias, Sun, Bitterroot, Flathead, Clark Fork, Musselshell

Wildlife: Black bears, grizzly bears, deer, bighorn sheep, elk, moose, antelope, wolves, mountain lions, mountain goats, wolverines, coyotes, beavers, bald eagles, hawks, owls, geese, ducks, many other kinds of birds, trout, perch, many other kinds of fish

Farm Products: Beef cattle, sheep, wheat, barley, milk, sugar beets, hogs, cherries, potatoes, hay

Mining Products: Coal, oil, copper, gold, silver, lead, platinum, talc, vermiculite, natural gas

Manufactured Products: Lumber, paper, other forest products, flour, meat, packaged sugar, other food products, concrete, metal products

Population: 799,065, forty-fourth among the states (1990 U.S. Census Bureau figures)

Major Cities (1990 state census figures):

Billings	81,151	Butte/Silver Bow	33,336
Great Falls	55,097	Helena	24,569
Missoula	42,918	Bozeman	22,660

Ponderosa pine

Montana History

About 8000 B.C.—Prehistoric Indians reach Montana

A.D. 1743—François and Louis Joseph de La Vérendrye, French-Canadian brothers, arrive in Montana

1776—The United States of America is founded

1803—The United States claims most of Montana through the Louisiana Purchase

1805—Sacagawea helps guide Lewis and Clark west through Montana

1806—The Lewis and Clark expedition comes back through Montana on its way east

1807—Manuel Lisa builds Montana's first fur-trading post

1841—Father Pierre-Jean De Smet builds St. Mary's Mission near present-day Stevensville

1846—Fort Benton is built

1862—Gold is discovered at Grasshopper Creek

1863—Virginia City is begun at the site of a gold strike

In 1864, Bannack (below) was the capital of the Montana Territory.

1864—Helena and Butte are founded as gold-mining towns; the Montana Territory is created

1875—Helena becomes the Montana Territory's capital

1876—The Sioux and Cheyenne kill George Custer and his troops in the Battle of the Little Bighorn

1877—Chief Joseph of the Nez Percé surrenders, ending Montana's Indian wars

1880—Nearly all of Montana's Indians are on reservations; the Utah and Northern Railroad reaches Montana

1889—Montana becomes the forty-first state

1895—The University of Montana opens in Missoula

1900—Montana's population is about 243,000

1910—Glacier National Park is created by the U.S. Congress

1917—Jeannette Rankin becomes the first woman member of the U.S. House of Representatives; a drought hits Montana

1917-18—More than 41,000 Montanans help the United States and its allies win World War I

1929—Another drought hits Montana; hard times last about ten more years

1934-40—About 10,000 workers build Fort Peck Dam

1935—Helena is rocked by earthquakes

1941-45—After the United States enters World War II, about 57,000 Montanans serve

1951—A large oil strike is made in eastern Montana

1959—An earthquake creates Quake Lake on the Madison River

1973—A new state constitution takes effect

1983—The Anaconda Company closes its mining operations in Butte

1989—Montana celebrates its one-hundredth birthday as a state

1990—Montana's population is 799,065

Stone markers at Custer Battlefield National Monument show where soldiers fell during the Battle of the Little Bighorn.

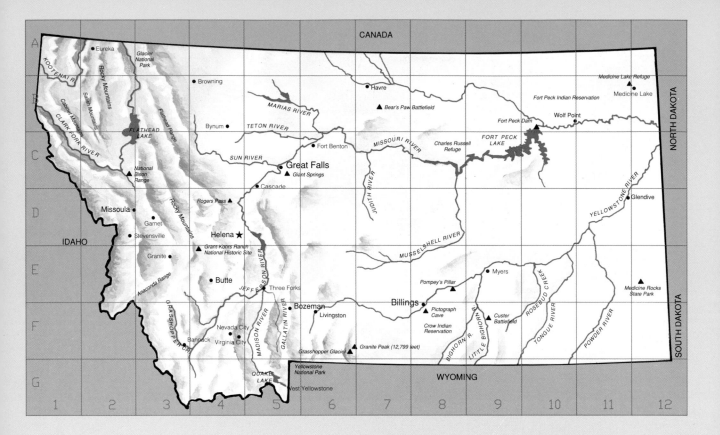

MAP KEY

60

GLOSSARY

ambassador: Someone who represents his or her government in another country

ancient: Relating to those living at a time early in history

artificial: Made by human beings; not natural

billion: A thousand million (1,000,000,000)

butte: A steep mountain or hill that rises sharply above the nearby land

canyon: A deep, steep-sided valley

capital: The city that is the seat of government

capitol: The building in which the government meets

climate: The weather of a region

Continental Divide: The North American highland that divides rivers that flow west into the Pacific Ocean from those that flow east into the Atlantic Ocean

dams: Barriers that hold back water

dinosaurs: Generally huge animals that died out millions of years ago

drought: A period when rainfall is well below normal in an area

explorers: People who travel in unknown lands to seek information

fossils: Remains of animals or plants that lived long ago

glaciers: Masses of slow-moving ice

herd: A group of animals that live together

independence: Freedom; the ability to take care of oneself

literacy: The ability to read and write

manufacturing: The making of products

million: A thousand thousand (1,000,000)

missionary: Someone who brings religion to people in faraway places

nugget: A solid lump or chunk of something

petrified wood: Wood that, over time, has turned to stone

pictographs: Drawings made on rock walls, usually in prehistoric times

plains: Generally flat, grassy lands

population: The number of people in a place

prehistoric: Belonging to the time before written history

rodeos: Contests in which cowboys and cowgirls ride horses and rope cattle

smallpox: A disease that once killed millions of people

spring: A place from which water comes out of a crack in the ground

surrender: To give up a fight

tepees: Tents made by North American Indians of the Great Plains

Tyrannosaurus rex: A huge meat-eating dinosaur

wildlife refuges: Places where animals are protected

PICTURE ACKNOWLEDGMENTS

Front cover, © SuperStock; 1, © Superstock; 2, Tom Dunnington; 3, © SuperStock; 4-5, Tom Dunnington; 6-7, © Stan Osolinski/Dembinsky Photo Associates; 8, courtesy of Hammond, Incorporated, Maplewood, New Jersey; 9 (left), © E. Cooper/H. Armstrong Roberts; 9 (right), © Tom Dietrich; 10, © Rob Outlaw; 11 (left), © Tom Dietrich/Tony Stone Worldwide/Chicago Ltd.; 11 (right), © Jerry Hennen; 12, © Chase Swift/Tom Stack & Associates; 13 (left), © Jerry Hennen; 13 (right), © Lynn M. Stone; 14, courtesy Sid Richardson Collection of Western Art, Fort Worth, Texas; 16 (top), Custer Battlefield National Monument; 16 (bottom), North Wind Picture Archives; 17, Historical Pictures Service, Chicago; 18, courtesy Sid Richardson Collection of Western Art, Fort Worth, Texas; 19 (top), North Wind Picture Archives; 19 (bottom), Montana Historical Society, Helena; 20 (top), © SuperStock; 20 (bottom), Montana Historical Society, Helena; 21, Museum of the Rockies; 23 (top), Historical Pictures Service, Chicago; 23 (bottom), Buffalo Bill Historical Center, Cody, Wyoming (detail; full picture appears in *America the Beautiful, Montana,* pp. 34-35); 24, Montana Historical Society, Helena; 25 (both pictures), Montana Historical Society, Helena; 26, Montana Historical Society, Helena; 27, Montana Historical Society, Helena; 29, © Diane Ensign Photo; 30, © Rob Stapleton/Dembinsky Photo Associates; 31, © Buddy Mays; 32, © Jerry Hennen; 33 (both pictures), © Tom Dietrich; 34-35, © M. Schneiders/H. Armstrong Roberts; 36, © Raymond G. Barnes/Tony Stone Worldwide/Chicago, Ltd.; 37 (left), © Tom Dietrich; 37 (right), © J. Wylder/Travel Montana Dept. of Commerce; 38, © Virginia R. Grimes; 39, © Diana Stratton/Tom Stack & Associates; 40, C. M. Russell Museum, Great Falls, Montana; 41, © Tom Dietrich; 42 (both pictures), © Jerry Hennen; 43 (left), © Tom Dietrich/Tony Stone Worldwide/Chicago, Ltd.; 43 (right), H. Hettick Photo/Travel Montana Dept. of Commerce; 44, © Rob Outlaw/Root Resources; 45 (left), © Tom Dietrich; 45 (right), © SuperStock; 46, © Virginia R. Grimes; 47, © Tom Dietrich; 48, UPI/Bettmann; 49, Historical Pictures Service, Chicago; 50, Historical Pictures Service, Chicago; 51, © Tom Dietrich; 52 (both pictures), AP/Wide World Photos; 53, Wide World Photos, Inc.; 54 (left), Rainbow Photo/Montana Tech Mineral Museum; 54-55 (tree), with the permission of Van Nostrand and Reinhold, *Volume 1, Illustrations for Architects, Designers, and Students,* by Larry Evans; 55 (right), Malmborg School; 56 (top), courtesy Flag Research Center, Winchester, Massachusetts 01890; 56 (middle), © Stan Osolinski/Dembinsky Photo Associates; 56 (bottom), © Rod Planck/Dembinsky Photo Associates; 57 (top), © Lynn M. Stone; 57 (bottom), © Jerry Hennen; 58, Museum of the Rockies; 59, © SuperStock; 60, Tom Dunnington; back cover, © Tom Dietrich

INDEX

Page numbers in boldface type indicate illustrations.

ABOUT THE AUTHORS

From Sea to Shining Sea: Montana is the first book Dennis and Judith Fradin have written together. The Fradins both graduated from Northwestern University in 1967. Dennis has been a professional writer for twenty years, and has published 150 books. His works for Childrens Press include the Young People's Stories of Our States series, the Disaster! series, and the Thirteen Colonies series. Judith earned her M.A. in literature from Northeastern University and taught high school and college English for many years. The Fradins, who are the parents of Anthony, Diana, and Michael, live in Evanston, Illinois.